CW00508276

CRICUT FOR BEGINNERS

All You Need To Know About Cricut, Expand On Your Passion For Object Design And Trasform Your Project Ideas From Thoughts To Reality

Melanie Williams

© Copyright 2021 Melanie Williams - All rights reserved.

The content contained within this book may not be reproduced, duplicated or transmitted without direct written permission from the author or the publisher. Under no circumstances will any blame or legal responsibility be held against the publisher, or author, for any damages, reparation, or monetary loss due to the information contained within this book. Either directly or indirectly.

Legal Notice

This book is copyright protected. This book is only for personal use. You cannot amend, distribute, sell, use, quote or paraphrase any part, or the content within this book, without the consent of the author or publisher.

Disclaimer Notice

Please note the information contained within this document is for educational and entertainment purposes only. All effort has been executed to present accurate, up to date, and reliable, complete information. No warranties of any kind are declared or implied. Readers acknowledge that the author is not engaging in the rendering of legal, financial, medical or professional advice. The content within this book has been derived from various sources. Please consult a licensed professional before attempting any techniques outlined in this book. By reading this document, the reader agrees that under no circumstances is the author responsible for any losses, direct or indirect, which are incurred as a result of the use of information contained within this document, including, but not limited to, - errors, omissions, or inaccuracies.

Table of Contents

INTRODUCTION 6
CHAPTER 1.   GETTING FAMILIAR WITH CRICUT 12
WHAT IS CRICUT? 12
CHAPTER 2.   MAINTAINING CRICUT 24
Maintaining the Cricut Machine 24
Maintaining the Cricut Cutting Mat 27
Maintaining the Cricut Cutting Blade 33
CHAPTER 3.   HOW TO START CRICUT 36
CRICUT SUGGESTIONS - TIPS THAT MAY HELP YOU TO GET STARTED 39
EARNING YOUR CRICUT MAT STICKY AGAIN 41
CHAPTER 4.   MATERIALS THAT CAN BE WORKED ON USING A
CRICUT MACHINE 44
MAIN MATERIALS 44
IRON-ON VINYL AND ADHESIVE VINYL 44
CARDSTOCK 45
PAPER 45
FABRIC 46
ALTERNATIVE MATERIALS 46
CHAPTER 5.   BASIC CRICUT MAKER TOOLS 50
SELECTING PENS TO USE 53
FINDING THE CURRENT FIRMWARE VERSION OF YOUR CRICUT MAKER 54
FINDING THE CURRENT DESIGN SPACE VERSION 55
HOW TO USE FAST MODE 56
CHOOSING A MATERIAL SETTING 57
CUSTOM CUT SETTINGS 58
CREATING CUSTOM SETTINGS 60
EDITING CUSTOM MATERIALS 61
REMOVING AND REPLACING ACCESSORY ADAPTERS 61
CHAPTER 6.   CRICUT PROJECT IDEAS TO TRY! 66
EASY PROJECTS 66
MEDIUM PROJECTS 70
DIFFICULT PROJECTS 73
CHAPTER 7.   HOW TO CONNECT CRICUT TO A COMPUTER 82
INSTALLING ON WINDOWS OR MAC 83
INSTALLING ON ANDROID OR IOS 85
CHAPTER 8.   THE BUSINESS SIDE OF THINGS AND IDEAS TO
EARN   88
CHAPTER 9.   CREATIVE IDEAS TO DO ON YOUR CRICUT 96
CONCLUSION 106

Introduction

The Cricut system is a famous invention. It's helped scrapbookers and lots of individuals with their demands not just restricted in the scrapbook creating planet but also to other aspects. However, it's to mention that one sector helped us in the scrapbooking kingdom. From the fantastic old dark ages, even if you weren't proficient at carvings or in case you didn't understand how to compose, your favorite moment goes down the drain.

Those two would be the sole means of maintaining the memories back afterward. It might appear crude and ancient to us back then; it was that they needed. Now, we've got everything set up to preserve someone's memories, and we all to Father Technology.

When a scrapbooker decides to make a scrapbook, the layout is almost always a key consideration. Before picking a design can cause migraines of epic proportions but today is another story. According to a particular pattern or layout, the Cricut system to be mentioned is only accountable for cutting edge newspapers, vinyl, and cloth. The design or print can make or edited using a software application known as the Cricut Design Studio.

Suppose you're searching for OK and straightforward - recognized designs that are already built-in. In that case, you proceed for capsules that are secondhand. There's no limit to everything you could think of using the layouts that already set up. The golden rule would be to allow your creativity to go crazy. It is a tool that any aspiring scrapbooker must possess. So far, is it? The prices generally start at $299 and will go up based on the version which you pick.

It might appear to be a substantial sum of money. However, the expense is well worth it. But if you wish to employ the additional effort to learn to locate a fantastic deal, you're more than welcome about this. The worldwide web is almost always a wonderful place to get some excellent bargains; you have to look. There is Amazon, eBay, so a lot more.

The Cricut machine has lots of uses besides being a cutter of layouts to get a scrapbook. The designs may use to make different things like greeting cards, wall decorations, and more. You simply have to believe creatively. There are no limitations, and when there are, they're only a figment of your imagination.

The Cricut Machine - A Short and Intimate Appearance

When you think about building a scrapbook, the first thing that comes in your head is what pictures to put. That is relatively simple as all you want to do would be to pick images that highlight a particular event or happening in your lifetime. After this complete, at this point, you should think of the layout of the scrapbook. Again, this can be quite simple as everything you have to do base your choice on whatever occasion has depicted in your pictures. Let us take, for instance, a wedding day.

Pick a design that will transfer that audience back in time and relive everything that transpired throughout your wedding day. Common sense is everything you may need here. How can you take action? Can you do it? No is the reply to those above query. You do so through the usage of a Cricut machine.

How exactly, how does one cost? Every unit comes with an average cost of $299, with more excellent versions having more massive price tags. However, there are means by which you'll be able to find a less high price. In case you've got a pc with the internet, proceed to browse and hunt for great bargains and inexpensive cutting machines that are secondhand.

Recall, nevertheless, that carrying purchases through eBay can take dangers, so that you need to be sure you check out each of the vendor's profiles, which you may want to participate in. Suppose you're the fantastic conventional shopper who'll never devote to internet purchasing. In that case, you could do this old - school and then buy from a mall through earnings or anything else similar.

The Cricut machine has additionally many applications that extend far beyond the domain of scrapbooking. Given the number of layouts in your cartridge or software application, you may always utilize them to make Cricut calendars, hangings such as partitions, and greeting cards for special events. Your creativity is the one thing that may limit your invention.

Marsha Brascher was crafting for several decades. She loves the challenge of producing cutting documents. She understands what is needed to make handmade crafts having the most complex of designs.

Cricut Suggestions - Tips That May Help You to Get Started

Capturing memories onto a virtual camera, even an HD camera, and a voice recorder make life much more purposeful. When there's a unique moment you would like to catch and be in a position to return to at any particular time, you can certainly do this so easily with the assistance of these instruments. However, pictures continue to be the favorite medium by the majority of people. If you wish to put together those images and compile them onto unique memorabilia, then you flip into scrapbooking.

Scrapbooking is a technique of preservation thoughts that's been in existence for quite some time, and it's evolved up to now better. With the creation of devices like the Cricut cutting edge machine, matters are made simpler. If you're Looking to Developing a scrapbook, this poor boy is the instrument for you. There Are Lots of good Cricut thoughts out there you can make the most.

Scrapbooks are only some of the many Cricut thoughts on the market. If you understand how to optimize it, this instrument makes it possible for you to create things that go past scrapbooking, for example, calendars. If you buy a Cricut cartridge, then there are a slew of layouts uploaded in every and every one. All these pre-made themes may use for a whole lot of items like hangings for partitions, image frames, picture frames, and greeting cards for many seasons.

Your creativity will limit your advancement using a Cricut machine. Together with calendars, you can design every month to represent the weather, the disposition, and exceptional events connected with that.

The Cricut machine will take care of this. But in case one cartridge doesn't have the layout that search, you may always go and purchase. It's that simple!

Cricut machines may be a little expensive, with all the cost starting at $299. That's pretty hefty for anybody to begin. Be a smart buyer. You may always turn into the World Wide Web to seek out incredible bargains on Cricut machines. Purchasing from eBay may also be a terrific move but can take several dangers if you experience eBay. In case you're quite worried about this, you always have the option to await a purchase to occur at one of the regional malls and buy out there since it will probably have a guarantee.

Chapter 1. Getting familiar with Cricut

What is Cricut?

For the Cricut, the common term is a die cutter, craft plotter, or smart cutter. This machine's architecture allows you to build projects from plain materials of varying thicknesses. Depending on your ability level with these products, the projects you can do with this tool will vary from easy to relatively complex. Your materials will vary from craft felt too thin sheets of metal, based on the sharpness of the blades in your cutting machine, or the model you are using. This gives you some idea of how large the selection is really for what this computer can help you accomplish as a crafter.

It's agreed to compile the best of what's available, so you don't have to sift through anything frustrating before you start making your glorious creations and enjoy your new Cricut computer. You will be able to access all the information you need about using the app in one unified location, project guides that take you from start to finish, a list of what you need, and so much more. This is your thorough guide, to which you can refer over and over, no matter how your level of ability increases over time.

We plan to offer you the most relevant information about Cricut, what it can do, how to take full advantage of your computer, and how to produce the best results consistently.

Let's dig into how to pick the right Cricut layout for you and your needs.

Choose the right model for you

Cricut's wonderful thing is that its models are all extremely flexible and competent. Some features one model has would cover the entire current Cricut product line. There are some very small variations in how they operate and the nature of their operation.

It listed all the models available at the moment from Cricut in the section below, what they do, how they vary, and which areas are better among certain models.

What's Available?

Luckily, at the time of writing, there aren't a huge number of art plotters available from Cricut, which means it'll be pretty quick for you to take a look at all the options without becoming frustrated. with huge product lines that contain many different models, it can be a real chore to find what you want and need while having the most for your money. There is a review of the currently available models below, what they can do, and what skills are better suited for what kind of crafts.

Cricut Explore One

This is the simplest machine they sell, in terms of what's currently available from Cricut. This machine boasts the ability to cut 100 of the most common materials available for use with your Cricut machine at the moment, as well as to be completely user friendly.

The Cricut Explore One is called the Cricut craft plotters no-frills beginner model and runs at a slower speed than the other available models. The Cricut Explore One has only one attachment clamp inside, so cutting or scoring cannot be performed simultaneously compared to the others available in the current model line. However, they can be done in quick succession, one directly after the other.

While this is a fantastic tool for a wide variety of crafts on 100 different materials and will get you on the right road to creating beautiful crafts that are often cut from others, the cost is not as high as you would think. If you're planning to use your art plotter exclusively for those special occasions where everything designed is perfect, then this is a great tool to have at hand.

Cricut Explore Air

Like all the Cricut Explore One and More features, the Cricut Explore Air model comes fitted like Bluetooth connectivity, has a built-in storage cup to hold your tools in one position while you're working, so they won't roll away or get lost in the shuffle.

This model does have two on-board accessory clamps which allow for marking and cutting or scoring simultaneously. Such clamps are labeled with an A and a B, so every time you put them up, you can be confident that your tools are going in the right places.

This model is designed to handle the same 100 materials as the Cricut Explore One and runs at the same pace, so the disparity in quality represents certain variations and similarities! It is a fantastic deal you're getting for the powerhouse.

Cricut Explore Air 2

The Cricut Explore Air 2 is the new top-selling craft plotter from Cricut and is arguably the best value for the quality they have to offer. This model cuts materials twice the two previous versions' speed, has Bluetooth compatibility, and the two adapter clamps on board.

The storage cup at the top of the unit features a smaller, shallower cut to store your new blade housings while they aren't in use. If you want to change for a project with many different tips, they're all readily accessible during your project. Both cups have a smooth silicone rim, so you won't have to worry about getting rusty or scratched at the blades on your computer!

This is the right equipment for the job for anyone who finds themselves using their Cricut at some regularity. You will be likely to do your crafts twice as quickly, and each time, even at that pace, you will get a satisfactory result!

Cricut Maker

The Cricut Creator is considered the flagship product of Cricut. It is the one that can do almost anything under the sun on just about any material that you can fit into your machine's mat guides. The one downside of this powerhouse model is its price point. It makes it model more prohibitive unless you intend to build crafts that you can sell using this model. If this is your goal, you can rest assured that the best of the best will be whatever you turn out with this machine every time. When you sell your art, this kid will pay for himself in little or no time at all.

This computer could be overkill for the amateur crafter's price who wants to turn up to the party with the most beautiful crafts that are leaps and bounds ahead of their peers. When you stick to the Joneses, of course, this is the style to have.

This model does have everything, and you can prove it. No other computer with Cricut has the pace the Cricut Creator has. The cuts that can be made with the unique precision blades that only suit this tool are crisper than anything that a straight knife or another design cutter could ever hope for. The blade housings enable you to simply remove the tip from the housing, mount the next one, re-clip it in place, and continue to roll through projects. The computer will identify the material loaded into it, so at the start of each of your projects, you won't need to specify the type of materials. One common occurrence with the other model is that the project is completed halfway before the crafter knows the dial is set incorrectly.

Unlike some others, the unit is completely capable of Bluetooth. It works with ten times as much power as some of the other versions. It has a special rotary cutter attachment allowing it to slice easily through fabrics with precision, and much more.

Are There Older Models?

Yeah. In a phrase. Some older models have been phased out to make way for the machines Explore and Builder. It was found that older machines need a lot more modifications, workarounds, troubleshooting, and comprehension to get precise or even squared cuts for the projects that artisans would like to do.

Here's a rundown of some of the versions you might have seen throughout your travels:

• Personal Cricut Digital Cutter Machine

• Cricut Create

• Expression 1

• Expression 2

• Imagine

• Cricut Mini

• Cricut Explore

These versions were compatible with a Cricut machine called the Gypsy, which was not unlike with the Cricut Design Space we currently have today. In innovating the methods of craft cutting, each of these machines had its triumphs.

Cricut wanted to change the key thing was the difficulty involved in dealing with their machines while making their newest line of products. Crafts societies had come together with hacks and math ledgers to configure their machines to function exactly as they wished.

With the current line of available models, the Cricut Design Room enables you to be as imaginative as you may be with the design process. None of your creative flow is absorbed by operations that your computer can take care of.

Updating is certainly worth the money if you own one of these machines, but if it has served you well in your manufacturing, there's no need to update. Cricut has always created quality products, and Cricut Design Space still supports cartridges containing different thematic design elements.

The Cricut Cartridge Adapter is a USB adapter enabling you to import your modules into the Cricut Design Space so that all of your elements are available in one organized room.

What are the Tools?

Cricut is a brand whose consumers listen. Due to that, they've thought of every possible resource you'd need to take the project from the very start, all the way to completion. I've compiled a list of all the tools to help you make your Cricut Design Space projects come true.

Browse at these things, get an idea of what they are, what they are doing, and you can see some of those right off the bat that can be replaced by other products that are not part of the Cricut brand.

You'll save time in doing so, and you might be able to make use of some of the devices you already have around your crafting station! Let's go dive in. Bonded Fabric Blades are made of German carbide steel for quick and precise cutting through bonded cloth. With the FabricGripTM pad, they can hold the fabric in place for the most accurate, cleanest cuts.

Both blades, and the housings that are also present for them, are specifically designed and built to suit the Cricut cutting machines Explore series, including the Explore Air models. The Cricut Maker needs a special kind of blade and space.

Craft Tweezers

Such reverse-action tweezers have a good grip, precise points, and after extended use, they relieve cramping. The ergonomic grip helps you to maintain a firm hold on your materials during the whole process, giving you the extra pair of hands, you'd always wish you had when you were made.

Cricut Explore® Wireless Bluetooth® Adapter

This product is designed to help your Cricut Explore and link to your computer or tablet using Bluetooth. Suppose you've invested in the

Cricut Explore One but find the Bluetooth features helpful. In that case, this handy adapter makes adding the feature to your Cricut Explore One computer easy to work with.

Deep-Point Replacement Blades

Deep-point blades allow you to easily make deeper, more accurate cuttings on even thicker materials. Over time, you can find the blades in accessory clamp B to get dull or simply become less precise. To resolve this, Cricut provides a line of replacement blades, and your blades will also react to sharpening a few times before replacement. Paper Crafting Set. You will find the edge distresser, quilling tool, piercing tool, and craft mat in this collection to be important in your crafts if you're really into papercraft. Quilling or paper filigree art is more common than ever, and these are some of the best tools available for that craft.

Portable Trimmer

This is an accuracy cutting tool that helps you cut your projects 100 percent of the time easily, crisply, and straight. They are especially common with scrapbookers. Many variations of this product are also on the market, and keep your eye out for those with positive reviews and a low price point.

Replacement Blades

There are replacement blades and housings on the current Cricut line, which are available for each model. Any blades that fit into the Cricut Explore One can fit into the Cricut Explore line any pattern. The blades for the Cricut Maker can suit for that particular model, so be sure to review the product details or packaging to make sure you have the correct blade for yourself.

Rotary Cutting Kit

This kit comes with a gridded cutting mat and a rotary cutting tool which always makes quick, straight, precise cuts. Cricut is far from the only manufacturer that sells a rotary cutting machine, so be sure to look at the product and price that's right for you in other products on the market.

Scissors

Every crafter knows that scissors are part and parcel of their tool kit. Although the scissors provided by Cricut are exceptionally sharp, with very fine dots on each blade, any pair suitable for your craft will help you well here.

Scoring Stylus

The scoring stylus is built to fit perfectly into your machine's Accessory Clamp A to score your projects to build and emboss impact, fold lines, and so much more. Also, the tool can be used freehand to produce the affects you want to produce in your art.

Scraper/Burnishing Tool

This basic tool should be your most-used Cricut tool, bar probably the weeding tool. You will find that once you raise your cut designs from the back layer, it will take gentle, steady pressure to burn your projects beautifully to move them to your project board. This tool can be replaced with other things in a pinch, but this tool does the best job.

Spatula

Often when you are peeling or setting out a project, you feel like you need an extra pair of hands. This tool gives you the extra support and maneuverability you need.

True Control™ Knife

It is a precision blade, similar in price and nature to XACTO. This knife is very useful for more accurate freehand cuts at any crafting station.

Weeding Tool

This is a hook with a very fine point, which helps you peel blanks from the vinyl you cut. For most, if not all, the projects that you do with your Cricut, this device will come in handy. It lets you remove the excess material from your design without having to bend, fold, or battle your material. This helps keep your template edges smooth, clean, and sharp whenever you like.

XL Scraper/Burnishing Tool

This offers an unbeatable degree of power. This exerts even pressure and helps remove uneven layering and bubbles in the air. The user community highly recommends this platform.

Paper Crafts Kit–In this package, you'll find the edge distresser, quilling tool, piercing tool, and craft pad to match your taste. Quilling or paper filigree art is becoming increasingly popular these days. These are some of the best resources available for that craft.

Chapter 2. Maintaining Cricut

I f you want your Cricut Machine to last for a very long time, you have to maintain it routinely. This means cleaning it properly and also maintaining the cutting mats and blades.

Maintaining the Cricut Machine

Over time, when using your Cricut machine, it will inevitably collect paper particles, dust, and debris. Also, grease in the device will begin to stick to the carriage track.

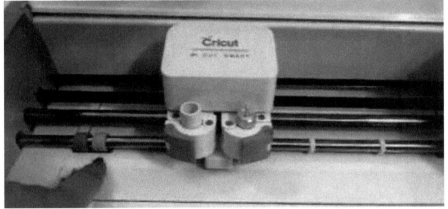

Photo credit: youtube.com

If you want your machine to last long, then you should clean it regularly, or else it can get damaged prematurely. Here are some cleaning tips to help you out when cleaning the machine.

- Before cleaning your machine, disconnect it from the power outlet. This will prevent electrocution or any other accident that can damage the device or injure you.

- When cleaning your machine, don't use any form of acetone. Acetone, like nail polish remover, will damage the plastic parts of the device permanently.

- You can clean the machine using a glass cleaner instead. Spray it on a clean, soft cloth and wipe the device gently.

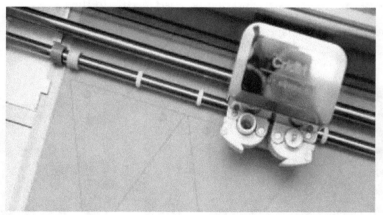

Photo credit: thewirecutter.com

- In the case of grease buildup on the carriage tracks, you should use a tissue, cotton swab, or soft, clean cloth to gently wipe it off.

- There is also the case of a buildup of static electricity on your machine. This can cause dust, debris, and particles to form on the device. This can also be easily cleaned with a soft, clean cloth.

Application of Grease for the Cricut Explore Models

- Disconnect the Cricut machine from the power outlet.

- Push the Cut Smart carriage gently to the left.

- Wipe the entire Cut Smart carriage bar with a tissue. The bar is the surface in front of the belt where the carriage slides on.

- Push the Cut Smart carriage gently to the right.

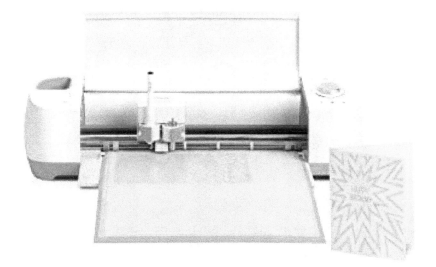

Photo credit: amazon.com

- Repeat the cleaning process for the other side by cleaning the bar with clean tissue.

- Then, push the Cut Smart carriage to the center of the bar.

- Take a lubrication packet, open it, and squeeze out a little grease. Put the amount of grease on a clean cotton swab.

- Apply a small coating of the grease on the two sides of the Cut Smart carriage around the bar to form a quarter inches ring on both sides.

- To make the grease become even in the carriage, push the Cut Smart carriage to the both sides slowly and repeatedly.

- Clean off any grease that stained the bar while you were greasing the machine.

- You can purchase a grease packet from Cricut. This will work better than using a third-party grease packet so that the machine will not get damaged. This is especially if, after using another grease product, your Cricut machine is making a grinding sound.

- This process is almost the same as greasing your Cricut Maker machine too.

Maintaining the Cricut Cutting Mat

You also have to clean and maintain your Cricut cutting mat because that is where the cutting occurs.

If the cutting mat isn't clean, it can stain the machine. Also, if your cutting mat has stopped sticking, it can spoil your designs and creations.

When your mat is no longer sticky because of debris and grime, cleaning it and making it sticky again will bring it back to life.

I will mention the solutions that are not ideal for the pink cutting mats, only for the green, blue, and purple.

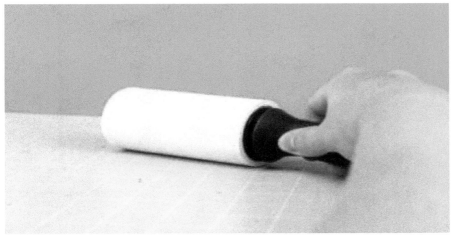

Photo credit: alittlecraftinyourday.com

There are many ways to clean your cutting mat.

- Using baby wipes:

Make use of alcohol-free, unscented, and bleach-free baby wipes to clean your mat. You should use the plainest baby wipes that you can find so that you don't add lotions, cornstarch, solvents or oils to your cutting mat. If not, you could affect the stickiness and adhesive of the mat. Also, after cleaning it, let it dry completely before using it.

- Using a Sticky Lint Roller

Photo credit: amazon.com

You can also use a roll of masking tape if you don't find a sticky lint roller. Run the roll across the mat to get rid of hairs, fibers, specks of dust, and paper particles.

This cleaning form can be done daily or between projects so that dust doesn't accumulate on the mat. This is a fast way to remove dirt apart from using tweezers or scrapers.

- Using warm water with soap

You can also clean the mat with soap and warm water. You should use the plainest soap possible too so that you don't mess with the mat. Use a clean cloth, sponge, soft brush, or a magic eraser. Also, rinse it thoroughly and don't use it until it is completely dry.

- Using an adhesive remover

In the case of heavy-duty cleaning, then you should use a reliable adhesive remover to clean it properly. When using an adhesive remover, read the directions properly before you start.

Then, spray a little amount on the mat and spread it around with a scraper or anything that can act as a makeshift scraper.

Photo credit: alittlecraftinyourday.com

Wait for a few minutes so that the solvent can work on the mat. Then, scrape the dirty adhesive off your mat with a scraper, paper towels, or cloth.

After this, wash the mat with warm water and soap if there is leftover residue and let it dry properly.

How to Make Your Cutting Mat Sticky Again

Photo credit: youtube.com

After washing or cleaning your cutting mat, you have to make them sticky again.

The most advisable way to make your mat sticky again is by adding glue to it. Get a solid glue stick like the Zig 2-Way Glue Pen and apply it on the mat's inner portion. Then, stroke the glue around the mat and ensure no glue residue on the edges of the mat.

After about 30 minutes, the glue will turn clear. Suppose the cutting mat turns out to be too sticky after you apply glue. In that case, you can use a piece of fabric to reduce the adhesive by pressing the material on the parts of the mat that are very sticky.

Cover the mat with a clear film cover after a few hours.

You can also use tacky glues or spray adhesives that are ideal for cutting mats.

General Maintenance

- When your mat isn't in use, cover it with a clear film cover so that dust and hairs won't accumulate on the surface of the mat.
- Handle your mats with care. If you want to ensure that the adhesive does not get damaged, avoid touching the sticky surface with your hands.

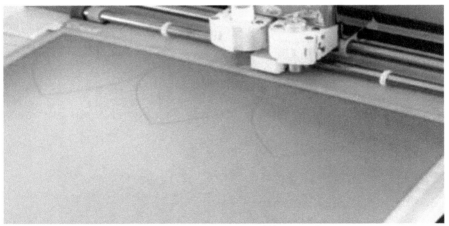

Photo credit: inspiration.cricut.com

Always ensure that your mat dries entirely before using it or covering it up. Don't use heat when drying your mat, but you can place it in front of a fan. Also, ensure that it is drying hanging up so that both sides will dry.

Maintaining the Cricut Cutting Blade

You can use your Cricut fine point blade for over a year if you maintain it properly! The same goes for the other types of cutting blades. When maintaining your Cricut cutting blade, you have to keep it sharp all the time so that it does not get worn out.

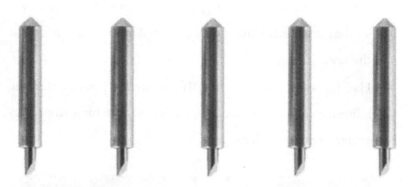

Photo credit: brandpost.co.nz

Keeping your blade sharp is essential because it can damage your materials and cause wastage if it isn't. Also, if you don't maintain your blades, you will have to replace them often.

Keeping Your Cutting Blade Sharp

- Spread a portion of an aluminum foil on a cutting mat. Without removing the blade from the housing, cut out a simple design in the foil. This will sharpen the blade and remove any paper particles, or vinyl stuck on the blade. This can be used for any type of cutting blade.

- In the case of heavy-duty cleaning, you should squeeze a sheet of aluminum foil into a ball. You need to remove the blade from the housing of the machine to use this method. Then, depress the plunger, take the blade, and repeatedly stick it into the aluminum foil ball. You can do this 50 times. This will make it sharper and also remove vinyl or paper particles on the blade.

How to Store Your Cutting Blade

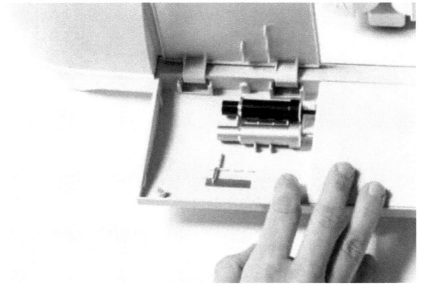

Photo credit: pinterest.com

The best way to store your cutting blade is to leave it in the Cricut compartment. You can place it in the drop-down door that is in front of the machine. That compartment is meant for storing the blade.

As for the blade housing, you can place it on the raised plastic points at the back of the machine. There are magnets in the front of the machine where you can stick loose blades.

When you put your blades in the Cricut machine, you never lose your blades.

Chapter 3.   How to Start Cricut

The Cricut system is a renowned invention. It helps scrapbookers and lots of individuals with their demands not just restricted in the scrapbook creating planet but also to other aspects. It is to be mentioned however that the 1 sector it is helped is on the scrap-booking kingdom. From the fantastic old dark ages, even if you were not proficient at carvings or in case you did not understand how to compose, your favourite moment goes down the drain.

Those two would be the sole means of maintaining the memories back afterward. It might appear crude and ancient to us back then; it was that they needed. Now, we have got everything set up to preserve someone's memories and, we all to Father Technology.

When a scrapbooker decides to make a scrapbook, that the layout is almost always a key consideration. Before, picking a design can cause migraines of epic proportions but today is another story. According to a particular pattern or layout, the cricut system to be mentioned is only accountable for cutting edge newspapers, vinyl, and cloth. The design or pattern can be made or edited using a software application known as the Cricut Design Studio.

Suppose you are searching for simple and well - recognized designs which are already built - in. In that case, you proceed for capsules that are secondhand. There is no limitation to everything you could think of using the layouts that are already set up. The golden rule would be to allow your creativity to go crazy. This is a tool which any aspiring scrapbooker must possess. So far is it? The prices generally start at $299 and will go up based on the version which you pick.

It might appear to be substantial sum of money; however, the expense is well worth it. But if you wish to employ the additional effort to learn to locate a fantastic deal, you are more than welcome about this. The world wide web is almost always a wonderful place to get some excellent bargains, you simply have to look. There is amazon, eBay, so a lot more.

The cricut machine has lots of uses besides being a cutter of layouts to get a scrapbook. The layouts may be used to make different things like greeting cards, wall decorations, and more. You simply have to believe creatively. There are not any limitations and when there are, they are only a figment of your imagination.

The Cricut Machine - A Short and Intimate Appearance

When you think about building a scrapbook, the very first thing comes in your head is exactly what pictures to put. That is fairly simple. All you want to do would be to pick images that highlight a particular event or happening on your lifetime. After this was completed, at this point you should think of the layout to the scrapbook. Again, this can be quite simple as everything you have to do is base your choice on whatever occasion has been depicted on your pictures. Let us take for instance, a wedding day.

Pick a design which will transfer that audience back in time and relive everything transpired throughout your wedding day. Common sense is everything you may need here. The next thing is to produce the layout. How can you act? Can you do it? No is the reply to those above queries. You do so through the usage of a cricut machine.

The cricut machine is a fantastic creation. This poor boy can help you cut paper, cloth, and vinyl sheets to whatever pattern you would like. These designs' actual production may be achieved via software tools like the cricut layout studio or via capsules using pre-engineered designs assembled into them. Therefore, if you are enthusiastic scrap booker, this system is essential have.

How exactly how does one cost? Well every unit comes with an average cost of $299 with greater versions having larger price tags. However there are means by which you will be able to find a less expensive price. In case you have got a pc with internet, proceed browse and hunt for great bargains and inexpensive cutting machines that are secondhand. eBay is a good place to begin with.

Recall nevertheless, that carrying purchases through eBay can take dangers so that you need to be certain you check out each of the vendor's profiles which you may want to participate in. Suppose you are the fantastic conventional shopper who will never devote to internet purchasing. In that case, you could do this old - school and then buy from a mall through earnings or anything else similar.

The cricut machine has additionally many applications which extend far beyond the domain of scrapbooking. Given the number of layouts in your cartridge or software application, you may always utilize them to make cricut calendars, hangings such as partitions, and greeting cards for special events. Your creativity is the one thing which may limit your creativity.

Marsha Brascher was crafting for several decades. She loves the challenge of producing cutting documents. She understands what is needed to make handmade crafts having the most complex of designs.

Cricut Suggestions - Tips That May Help You to Get Started

Capturing memories onto a virtual camera, even an HD camera, and a voice recorder make life much more purposeful. When there is a unique moment you would like to catch and be in a position to return to at any certain time, you can certainly do this so easily with these instruments' assistance. However, pictures continue to be the favorite medium by the majority of people. If you wish to put together those images and compile them onto distinctive memorabilia, then you flip into scrapbooking.

scrapbooking is a technique of preservation of thoughts that has been in existence for quite some time and it is evolved up to now better. Previously, the invention of a single scrapbook was a monumentally crazy job. With the Creation of devices like the Cricut cutting edge machine, matters are made simpler. If you are Looking to Developing a scrapbook, this poor boy is the instrument for you. There Are Lots of good cricut thoughts out there you can make the most of.

Scrapbooks are only some of many cricut thoughts on the market. If you understand how to optimize it, this instrument makes it possible for you to create things that go past scrapbooking for example calendars. If you buy a cricut cartridge, then there is a slew of layouts uploaded in every and everyone. All these pre- made themes may be used for a whole lot of items like hangings for partitions, image frames, picture frames, and greeting cards for many seasons.

Just your creativity will limit your advancement using a cricut machine. Together with calendars, you can design every month to represent the weather, the disposition, and exceptional events connected with that. The cricut machine will take care of this. But if one cartridge does not have the layout that search, you may always go and purchase. It is that simple!

Cricut machines may be a little expensive with all the cost starting at $299. That is pretty hefty for anybody to begin with. Be a smart buyer. You may always turn into the world wide web to seek out great bargains on cricut machines. Purchasing from eBay may also be a terrific move. Still, it can take several dangers if you are not experienced with eBay. In case you are quite worried about this, you always have the option to await a purchase to occur at one of the regional malls and buy out there since it will probably have a guarantee.

Those are among the numerous great cricut thoughts on the market. Calendars so many more could be made with the usage of this machine that is fantastic. Bear in mind, only your imagination will restrict what you could do.

Earning Your Cricut Mat Sticky Again

Are you aware you do not have to obtain a new mat every-time your mat reductions are stickiness?

When your mat reaches the point at which nothing will adhere and your newspaper only moves around if you attempt to reduce, then it is time to "re-stickify" (is that a phrase??) Your mat. This is a straightforward procedure and you will be stunned at how well it is working!

Step 1- Carry your mat into your sink. Utilize some hot water, a couple drops of dish soap and a green scotch brite washing machine. Scrub your carpet beneath the tepid water. You will begin to find the small pieces of newspaper and filthy sticky grime begin to come off. You might even utilize the scrapper which came on the Cricut tool kit that will assist you scrap away some of the gunk also. Keep scrubbing before all of that additional layer of gunk is eliminated. Based upon your mat, then this can strip it all of the way to the vinyl with no stickiness left or right there can still be a little quantity of stickiness. Either way would be acceptable.

Step 2- You then wish to let it airdry or use your own hair dryer. Do not use a towel to wash it since it is going to leave lint.

Step 3- Permit that airdry for approximately one hour. It is ready to rock & roll up back again. I have done this on my mats and over again.

Measure 4- Then, have a wide tipped ZIG 2-way glue pen and use paste in lines round the entire mat.

Measure 5- Permit dry for 1 hour before implementing the translucent sheet back.

Chapter 4. Materials That Can Be Worked on Using a Cricut Machine

When you look at what Cricut makers can do, you're going to realize there are a ton of materials to choose from. But, which ones do you really need? Which ones are kind of useless? Well, here are some of the primary materials you should consider buying, and the materials that you don't necessarily need when using your Cricut machine.

Main Materials

Iron-On Vinyl and Adhesive Vinyl

This is one of the best materials for a Cricut blade, especially fine-point Cricut blades. You can adjust the settings and design the image onto the vinyl. Then, by ironing it on or using the Cricut press, you can create shirts and other appliques for outfits. You'll want to make sure that the iron-on setting is on your Cricut, however, before you think about using this.

You will realize that when you start to look for vinyl, the ideal type to choose is heat-transfer vinyl since you can simply iron or press it on. There are many different options, including fuzzy locked or glitter vinyl, that you can purchase.

Adhesive vinyl is another good one, and there are many different ways to use this. Containers, ornaments, and the like benefit immensely from this material. You can get permanent outdoor and removable indoor options. Again, Cricut machines are known for cutting vinyl, and this material is worth it if you're thinking about making decals, as well.

Cardstock

If you're doing any scrapbooking or making cards, you'll want to consider crafting your items with cardstock. You can choose some tremendous 65-pound cardstock for your crafting projects, and the nice part about this option is that it's pretty cheap.

Paper

Cereal boxes, construction paper, embossed paper, even freezer paper can be used with your Cricut machine. Some users have had a lot of luck with the poster board, too, but you'll want to make sure you clean your blades if you plan on using this material since the poster board can be quite trying on them. Your blades could end up dulling over time, so make sure you clean them with aluminum foil.

Craft paper is another option, as well, and if you're creating personalized boxes, this is an excellent material to consider – it can help bring a more personalized touch to your finished product.

Fabric

With some fabrics, you'll need a lighter grip board, such as for silk or polyester, but if you're working with heavy materials such as leather, burlap, or canvas, make sure that you have StrongGrip cutting boards. But the fabric is another great option for your Cricut experience, since they are lovely for cutting materials, and fabrics can also be printed on. You will want to make sure you use a stabilizer, such as Heat N Bond or Wonder Under before you cut them, to prevent the fabric from getting messed up. Different cuts can be made to fabric and textiles with the Cricut Explore machine. Cricut maker machines work best with material, though there is the consideration that it could be a bit pricey.

Alternative Materials

While those are the primary materials, you also have some other alternative options. If you're working with light fabric, typically the Explore series of machines are ideal.

One great material you could try is the chipboard. If you're working with a chipboard thicker than what your blades can handle, then you can insert the material into the Cricut machine and let it work its magic.

Rubber is another option that a lot of people don't think about when they're using a Cricut machine. If you're trying to create custom-designed stamps, such as for pottery or other projects, consider this option. You'll want a deep-cut blade for this, but it works.

Wood veneer works well with your Cricut machine, but you'll want to make sure that you have both a fine-point and a deep-point blade, depending on the project. This material will also take a little longer to cut.

What about magnets? That's right, you can make your own customized magnets with a Cricut machine. These are great for gifts for teachers or friends, and the best part is you don't have to sit around, trying to cut out intricate designs on your own. They're lovely and super fun.

Craft foam is really good for arts and crafts with children, but if you don't want to spend all your time cutting out various shapes for the kids to use, just insert the design into the Cricut machine and let it do the work. This is wonderful for art teachers who want to put together a project but don't want to deal with the hassle of spending all their time prepping the materials.

Finally, you have a mat board. This will require a deep-point blade, but if you want a strong material for a durable art project, this is a wonderful option.

The craziest part of Cricut machines is that it can cut items you wouldn't ever expect – tissue paper, stencil paper to make your own stencils, sticker paper to make stickers, plastic packages, adhesive foil, and even aluminum foil can be used with this! So, yes, there are so many options for your Cricut experience and so many designs that you can take advantage of that it's worth checking out, that's for sure.

To put it simply, Cricut machines can handle a ton of materials. The general idea is that if the machine can cut it, chances are you can use it, so don't be afraid to try some of your crazy ideas – Cricut machines are quite wonderful for just about everything.

Chapter 5. Basic Cricut Maker Tools

These are the essential tools you will need for simple projects. There are several other tools that you can use for specialized tasks that can be purchased subsequently. Here is a collection of essential tools you will need to get started on your craft making journey.

Knife Blade & Housing

This blade is particularly useful for cutting wood and materials that are up to 2mm thick. They are excellent for projects involving wood and similarly hard materials. This blade wears out after a few times of use. There are replacement blades you can buy which work fine.

Scoring Stylus

The scoring stylus helps you make accurate fold lines and creases on your material.

Rotary Blade

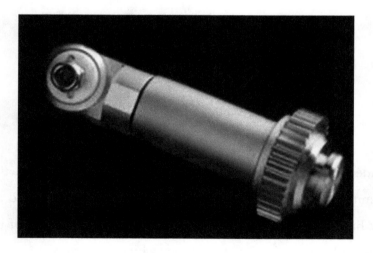

This is a special blade that works excellently with fabrics.

Premium Fine Point Blade

This blade comes in the Fine Point Blade housing already installed in your machine. It works well with Vinyl and paper materials, cutting them easily without any issues. Unlike the knife blade, the fine point blade does not easily wear out and is long-lasting.

Scraper and Spatula

The scraper and the spatula help you take off materials from the cutting mat.

Weeding Tool

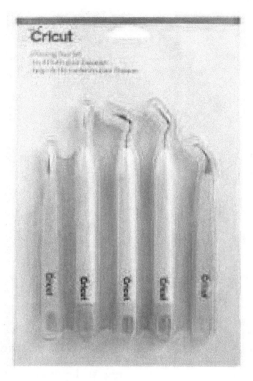

This tool helps you take off pieces of cut materials that are stuck on the cutting mat. The tool sometimes comes in a complete tool kit.

Selecting Pens to Use

The Cricut Maker allows you to use pens to write and draw simultaneously. The pens are non-toxic and are permanent once they get dry. The pens differ in tip size and create different effects. The type of pen you select should depend on what effect you want to create.

• There are calligraphy tip pens with tips ranging from 0.2 to 2.0 in size. You can check the Black Set, it a good calligraphy pen set.

• The Metallic Pen Set is also another pen set. They work well on card stock paper. You have a variety of colors with the metallic pen set.

• There is the Classic Pen set which gives off a regular pen effect.

• The Glitter Bright Set gives the glitter effect.

Finding the current firmware version of your Cricut Maker

You can find out the firmware version of your Cricut Maker using these steps.

1. Switch on your Cricut Maker and connect it to your computer.
2. Login to your Cricut Design Space account.

3. Click on the Account menu (≡). It is on the top left corner of the screen.

4. Select Update Firmware.

5. A list of machines will drop down. Select Cricut Maker from the list.

6. The computer will detect your machine. If your firmware is up to date, you will be notified. If it is not, you will be asked to update it. The latest Cricut Maker firmware version, for now, is 4.175.

Note: You can only use a computer (Mac or Windows) to check the firmware version of your Cricut Maker. You cannot use the apps (iOS or Android) to check it.

Finding the current Design Space Version

For Windows Computers

1. Select the arrow on the taskbar to open hidden icons.

2. Allow your mouse pointer to hover over the Design Space icon.

3. The plugin version will appear.

Checking Design Space Version for Mac

1. Click on the Cricut icon. It is found at the top right end of the screen.

2. Click on "About."

3. A small window pops up showing information that includes the current version.

How to use Fast Mode

The Fast Mode is a feature limited to Cricut Explore Air 2 and Cricut Maker machines. This feature allows you to cut and write at speeds that are up to two times the normal cutting and writing speeds. You can use the fast mode on Cardstock materials, Vinyl, and Iron-on materials.

Here is how you turn on Fast Mode on your mobile device and computer

●   When you are about to write or cut the material, move to the Cut screen.

●   Having selected the materials to be cut in the previous screen, the Fast Mode option will appear.

●   Turn on the Fast Mode option

The image below illustrates the process.

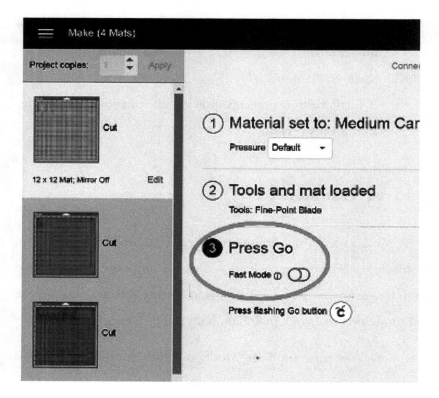

Note: It is normal for your Cricut Maker to make noise that is louder than usual when cutting or writing in Fast Mode.

Choosing a Material setting

The Cricut Maker has pre-set settings that guarantee the best results on defined materials. With the Smart Set Dial, you do not have any business with speed, or pressure settings all you do is to turn the dial to the right material and push the Go button.

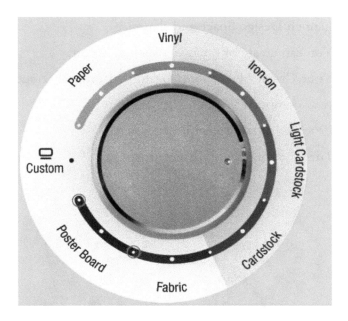

There are pre-loaded settings for materials like Paper, Vinyl, Iron-on, Light Cardstock, Cardstock, Fabric, and Poster Board. After working on Design Space and making your settings there, you simply turn the dial to the material you wish to work with. For instance, you wish to cut Vinyl, after making all the settings on Design Space, you turn the dial on the Smart Set Dial to Vinyl before you push Go to begin cutting.

Custom Cut Settings

Your Cricut Maker cuts more than just seven types of materials. To give more flexibility, there are several other materials settings you can access via Design Space. This gives you more precise cutting settings. Here is how to use Custom Cut settings.

1. Launch Design Space and sign in.

2. You can create or open an existing project.

3. Your Cricut Maker must be turned on and connected to your computer.

4. Proceed to the Project Preview screen.

5. Turn the smart set Dial to Custom

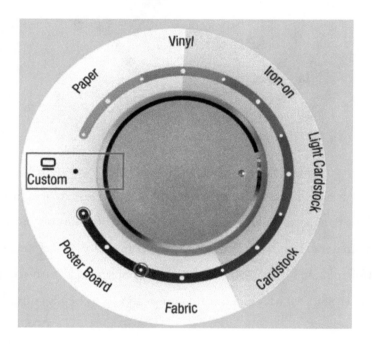

6. Click on Browse All Materials.

7. A drop-down list will appear with the names of materials. Select the material you wish to work with.

Creating Custom Settings

Sometimes the custom settings available may not come close enough to the material you want to cut. You can, however, create your custom material that can be as close as possible to the material you wish to cut. Here is how it is done.

1. Go to Menu (☰)
2. Select Manage Custom Materials or select Material Settings.
3. Scroll down to the bottom of the page and click on Add New Material.
4. Create a name for your new material and click Save.
5. With the new material saved, you can adjust the following parameters for cutting the material:

▪ Cut Pressure- This is the pressure with which the machine cuts the material. You can use the sliders to adjust this.

▪ Multi-cut – This makes the machine cut over the same object several times. It works well with thick materials.

▪ Blade Type

6. Click Save to save your new material.
7. The new material will now be available in the list of materials.

Editing Custom materials

To edit or delete a custom material you have created.

1. Launch the Menu (≡)

2. Select Manage Custom Materials.

3. Select the material

4. Click the Edit button

5. Edit as appropriate or Click on

Delete.

Removing and Replacing Accessory Adapters

Here is how to replace accessory adapters safely.

1. Open the accessory Clamp A.

2. Put your thumb under the accessory adapter and put pressure from under while you push down from the top with your other fingers. The adapter will come out of the clamp.

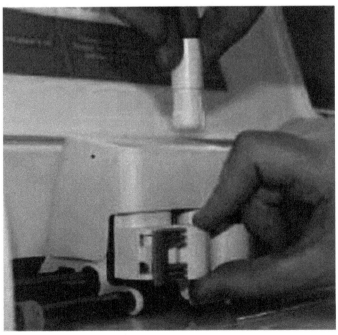

3. To put back an accessory adapter, place your finger under the clamp to steady it and put it in the adapter from the top.

4. Apply gentle pressure until the adapter snaps into place.

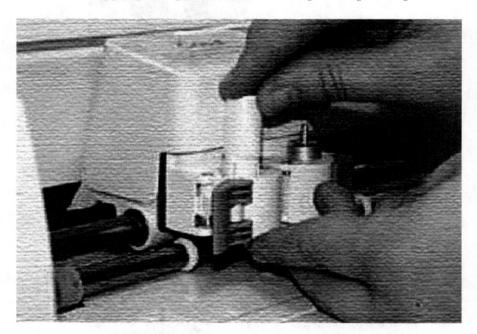

Cricut Maker Project Ideas

There are several amazing things you can do with your Cricut Maker. Are you having a hard time with project ideas? Here are a few to get you started.

1. Vinyl Decals and Stickers

2. Sewing Patterns

3. Homemade Cards

4. Christmas tree ornaments

5.   Jigsaw Puzzles

6.   T-Shirt transfers

7.   Baby Clothes

8.   Felt Toys

9.   Wedding Invitations

10.   Fabric Keyrings

11.   Halloween Decorations

12.   Iron-on Vinyl work

13.   Cake Toppers

14.   Gift Tags

15.   Pin Cushions

A few of these projects will be further explained subsequently in this book.

Chapter 6. Cricut Project Ideas to Try!

With Cricut, the ideas for projects are so vast, you'll be amazed at how much you can do. So, what are some ideas that could work for you? Here are a few that you can consider, and some of the best project ideas for those who are stumped on where to begin!

Easy Projects

Custom Shirts

Custom shirts are incredibly easy. The beauty of this is, you can use the Cricut fonts or system options, and from there, you can simply print it on. Personally, I like to use the iron-on vinyl, because it's easy to work with. Just take your image and upload it into Design Space. Then, go to the canvas and find the image you want. Once you've selected the image, you click on the whitespace that will be cut – remember to get the insides, too. Make sure that you choose cut image, not print from cut image, and then place it on the canvas to the size of your liking. Put the iron-on vinyl shiny side down, turn it on, and then select iron-on from the menu. Choose to cut, and make sure you mirror the image. Once done, pull off the extra vinyl to remove the vinyl between the letters. There you go! A simple shirt.

Vinyl Decals

Vinyl can also be used to make personalized items, such as water bottle decals. First, design the text – you can pretty much use whatever you want for this. From here, create a second box and make an initial, or whatever design you want. Make sure that you resize this to fit the water bottle, as well.

From here, load your vinyl, and make sure that you use transfer tape on the vinyl itself once you cut it out. Finally, when you adhere the lettering to the bottle, go from the center and then push outwards, smoothing as you go. It takes a bit, but there you have it – simple water bottles that children will love! This is a wonderful, simple project for those of us who aren't really that artistically inclined but want to get used to making Cricut items.

Printable Stickers

Printable stickers are the next project. This is super simple and fun for parents and kids. The Explore Air 2 machine works best.

With this one, you want the print then cut feature, since it makes it much easier. To begin, go to Design Space and download images of ice cream or whatever you want, or upload images of your own. You click on a new project, and on the left side that says images, you can choose the ones you like, and insert more of these on there.

From here, choose the image and flatten it, since this will make it into one piece rather than just a separate file for each. Resize as needed to make sure that they fit where you're putting them.

You can copy/paste each element until you're done. Once ready, press saves, and then choose this as a print then cut image. Click the big button at the bottom that says make it. Make sure everything is good, then press continue, and from there, you can load the sticker paper into the machine. Make sure to adjust this to the right setting, which for sticker paper is the vinyl set. Put the paper into there and load them in, and when ready, the press goes – it will then cut the stickers as needed.

From there, take them out and decorate. You can use ice cream or whatever sticker image you want!

Personalized Pillows

Personalized pillows are another fun idea and are incredibly easy to make. To begin, you open up Design Space and choose a new project. From here, select the icon at the bottom of the screen itself, choosing your font. Type the words you want, and drag the text as needed to make it bigger.

You can also upload images, too, if you want to create a huge picture on the pillow itself.

From here, you want to press the attach button for each box, so that they work together and both are figured when centered, as well.

You then press make it – and you want to turn to mirror on, since this will, again, be on iron-on vinyl. From here, you load the iron-on vinyl with the shiny side down, the press continues, follow the prompts, and make sure it's not jammed in, either.

Let the machine work its magic with cutting and from there, you can press the weeding tool to get the middle areas out.

Set your temperature on the easy press for the right settings, and then push it onto the material, ironing it on and letting it sit for 10 to 15 seconds. Let it cool, and then take the transfer sheet off.

There you have it! A simple pillow that works wonders for your crafting needs.

Cards!

Finally, cards are a great project idea for Cricut makers. They're simple, and you can do the entire project with cardstock.

To make this, you first want to open up Design Space, and from there, put your design in. If you like images of ice cream, then use that. If you want to make Christmas cards, you can do that, too. Basically, you can design whatever you want to on this.

Now, you'll then want to add the text. You can choose the font that you want to use, and from there, write out the message on the card, such as "Merry Christmas." At this point, instead of choosing to cut, you want to choose the right option – the make it option. You don't have to mirror this, but check that your design fits properly on the cardstock itself. When choosing material for writing, make sure you choose the cardstock.

From there, insert your cardstock into the machine, and then, when ready, you can press go and the Cricut machine will design your card. This may take a minute, but once it's done, you'll have a wonderful card in place. It's super easy to use.

Cricut cards are a great personalized way to express yourself, creating a one-of-a-kind, sentimental piece for you to gift to friends and family.

Medium Projects

Cricut Cake Toppers

Cricut cake toppers have a little bit of added difficulty because they require some precise scoring. The Cricut maker is probably the best piece of equipment for the job, and here, we'll tell you how to do it. The scoring tool is your best bet since this will make different shapes even easier, as well. You will want to make sure you have cardstock and the cutting mat, along with a fine-point blade for cutting. The tape is also handy for these.

First, go to Design Space and choose the rosettes you want. From there, the press makes it and follow the prompts. It will then ask you whether you want the single or double wheel. Scoring shells are meant to create extra-deep score lines in materials, to get the perfect fold. The single wheel will make one crease, and the double wheel will make a parallel wheel that will crease – perfect for specialty items. Plus, the double wheel is thicker, so it's easier to fold.

Once you score everything, you remove it and replace the scoring wheel with the fine-point blade.

From here, you simply fold everything and just follow the line. This should make the rosette, and you can then use contrasting centers and create many of these to form a nice backdrop.

Cricut Gift Bags

Next, are gift bags. Remember to put the foil poster board face-down on the mat itself, to help prevent the material from cracking and showing through to the white backdrop, when you fold them together after you score them.

To make these, you want to implement the template that you'd like to use in Design Space. From here, I do suggest cutting out the initial design first, and then putting it back in to create scoring lines, following the same steps. After that, you can then take your item and fold along the score lines, and then use adhesive or glue to help put it all together. This is a great personalized way to do it but can be a bit complicated to work with at first.

Cricut Fabric Coasters

Fabric coasters with a Cricut maker are great, and they need only a few supplies. These include the maker itself, cotton fabric, fusible fleece, a rotary cutting mat or some scissors, a sewing machine, and an iron.

Cut the fabric to about 12 inches to fit the cutting mat – if it's longer, you can hang it off, just be careful.

From here, go to Design Space, then click shapes and make a heart. You can do this with other shapes, too. Resize it to about 5 inches wide. Press make it, and you'll want to make sure you create four copies. Press continue, and then choose medium fabrics similar to cotton. You then load the mat and cut, and then you do it again with the fusible fleece on the cutting mat, changing it to 4.75 inches. This time, when choosing the material, go to more, and then select fusible fleece. Cut the fusible fleece, and then attach these to the back of the heart with the iron and repeat with the second.

Sew the two shapes together, leaving a gap for stitching and the turning. Clip the curves, turn it inside out, and then fold in the edges and stitch it.

There you go – a fusible fleece heart coaster. It's a little bit more complicated, but it's worth trying out.

Difficult Projects

Giant Vinyl Stencils

Vinyl stencils are a good thing to create, too, but they can be hard. Big vinyl stencils make for an excellent Cricut project, and you can use them in various places, including bedrooms for kids.

You only need the explore Air 2, the vinyl that works for it, a pallet, sander and, of course, paint and brushes. The first step is preparing the pallet for painting, or whatever surface you plan on using this for.

From here, you create the mermaid tail (or any other large image) in Design Space. Now, you'll learn immediately that big pieces are hard to cut and impossible to do all at once in Design Space.

What you do is section of each design accordingly, and remove any middle pieces. Next, you can add square shapes to the image, slicing it into pieces so that it can be cut on a cutting mat that fits.

At this point, you cut out the design by pressing make it, choosing your material, and working in sections.

From here, you put it on the surface that you're using, piecing this together with each line, and you should have one image after piecing it all together. Then, draw out the line on vinyl and then paint the initial design. For the second set of stencils, you can simply trace the first one and then paint the inside of them. At this point, you should have the design finished. When done, remove it very carefully.

And there you have it! Bigger stencils can be a bit of a project since it involves trying to use multiple designs all at once, but with the right care and the right designs, you'll be able to create whatever it is you need to in Design Space so you can get the results you're looking for.

Cricut Quilts

Quilts are a bit hard to do for many people, but did you know that you can use Cricut to make it easier? Here, you'll learn an awesome project that will help you do this. To begin, you start with the Cricut Design Space. Here, you can add different designs that work for your project. For example, if you're making a baby blanket or quilt with animals on it, you can add little fonts with the names of the animals, or different pictures of them, too. From here, you want to make sure you choose the option to reverse the design. That way, you'll have it printed on correctly. At this point, make your quilt. Do various designs and sew the quilt as you want to.

From here, you should cut it on the iron-on heat transfer vinyl. You can choose that, and then press cut. The image will then cut into the piece.

At this point, it'll cut itself out, and you can proceed to transfer this with some parchment paper. Use an EasyPress for best results and push it down. There you go, an easy addition that will definitely enhance the way your blankets look.

Cricut Unicorn Backpack

If you're making a present for a child, why not give them some cool unicorns? Here is a lovely unicorn backpack you can try to make. To make this, you need ¾ yards of a woven fabric — something that's strong, since it will help with stabilizing the backpack. You'll also need half a yard of quilting cotton for the lining. The coordinating fabric should be around about an eighth of a yard. You'll need about a yard of fusible interfacing, some strap adjuster rings, a zipper that's about 14 inches and doesn't separate, and some stuffing for the horn.

To start, you'll want to cut the main fabric, and you should use straps, the loops, a handle, some gussets for a zipper, and the bottom and side gussets.

The lining should be done, too, and you should make sure you have the interfacing. You can use fusible flex foam, too, to help make it a little bit bulkier.

From here, cut everything and then apply the interfacing to the backside, and the flex foam should be adjusted to achieve the bulkiness you are looking for. You can trim this, too. The interfacing should be one on the backside, and then add the flex foam to the main fabric. The adhesive side of this will be on the right-hand side of the interfacing.

Fold the strap pieces in half and push one down, on each backside. Halve it, and then press it again, and stitch these closer to every edge, and also along the short-pressed edge, as well.

From here, do the same thing with the other side but add the ring for adjustment, and stitch the bottom of these to the main part of the back piece.

Then add them both to the bottom.

At this point, you have the earpieces that you should do the backside facing out. Stitch, then flip out and add the pieces.

Add these inner pieces to the outer ear, and then stitch these together.

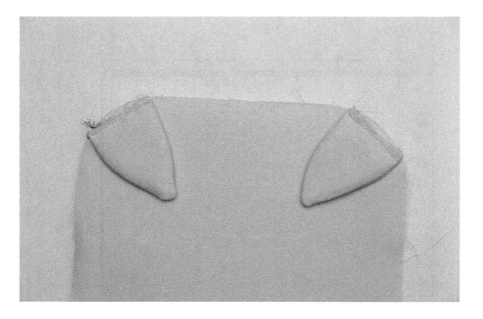

At this point, you make the unicorn face in the Design Space. You'll notice immediately when you use this program everything will be black, but you can change this by adjusting the desired layers to each color.

You can also just use a template that fits, but you should always mirror this before you cut it.

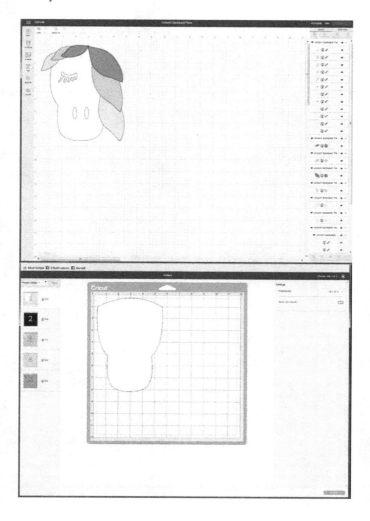

Choose vinyl, and then insert the material onto the cutting mat. From there, cut it and remove the iron-on slowly.

You will need to do this in pieces, which is fine because it allows you to use different colors. Remember to insert the right color for each cut. At this point, add the zipper, and there you go!

Diamond Planters

Finally, we have some diamond planters. These are a bit complicated, but there is a pattern to do it. Essentially, you create the diamond design and the trapezoids on top and then cut them into the chipboard. Make sure to choose a chipboard in your materials. From there, cut them, and then use masking tape to hold these pieces as you glue. When done, you essentially do the same with the trapezoid pieces and put them on top. Then, just get the outside seams. Once dried, remove the tape. This project is more complicated due to the extra steps you need to take with assembling it and getting the Cricut measurements right.

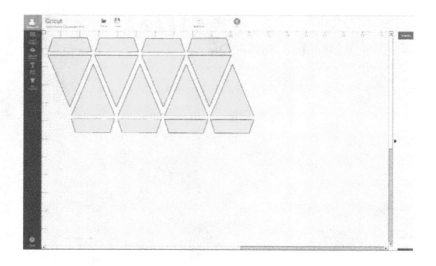

Cricut projects are fun, and with the instructions in this section of the book, you should have everything you need to get started with some of the easier, more popular projects. There are tons more out there to choose from, so once you've got a handle on the ones we've suggested, take a look and see what else you might be interested in creating. Your options are almost limitless, thanks to your Cricut machine.

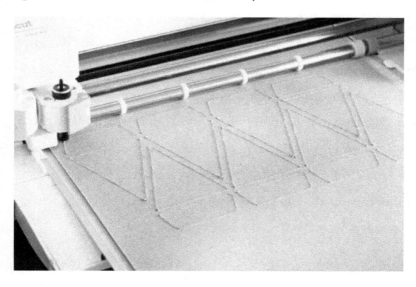

Chapter 7. How To Connect Cricut To A Computer

The excitement of getting your brand new Cricut Machine is unique. It's not every day that you can get a machine that's as powerful as the Cricut Machine, well, at least as far as home DIY projects go. It is something that is both exciting and challenging. It assures that you are looking to get started as soon as possible. But before you can get your hands dirty, you need to set up your Cricut Machine.

Fortunately, Cricut has made it easy to set up your Cricut Machine. If you've ever installed a printer or any other external device on your computer, then you will find it easy to install your very own Cricut Machine.

There is just one crucial recommendation before making the installation: please ensure that you can devote the time needed to get the machine running. So, please take your time; it doesn't work at first. The last thing you want is to rush through the installation process. While it's pretty straightforward, there are times when running through installation; you might miss a step that keeps the device from working. It is what we are looking to avoid.

Installing On Windows Or Mac

To kick things off, we're going to look at how to install on a laptop or PC. You will find that installing the Cricut Machine on a computer or PC is just like setting up a printer. It's a pretty straightforward deal. So, do keep in mind that you will need about 15 or 20 minutes to get through the entire installation process.

Here is a breakdown of the steps needed to get the Cricut Machine up and running.

1. Check power. Firstly, plug your Cricut Machine and press the on button. It is essential, especially in the rare event that the machine defective. Otherwise, you might struggle to try to get the installation done with an unresponsive device.

2. Connect the machine to your computer. Secondly, connect your device to your laptop or PC. There are two ways to do this, using the USB cord (it provides in the kit, or you can also use one from a printer) or via Bluetooth. With the power cord, it's just a question of plugging it in, and that's that. If you choose to connect via Bluetooth, enable your computer's Bluetooth connection and then pair with the Cricut Machine.

3. You are going to the Cricut website. This step is essential, especially if you are setting up a machine for the first time. Go to design.cricut.com/setup on your browser. You'll be directed to the Cricut website and then prompted to create your Cricut ID.

4. Create your Cricut ID. At this point, you'll prompt by a set of instructions. Follow these instructions to create your Cricut ID. Now, if you already have a Cricut ID, then you can skip this step. Nevertheless, if you are installing a brand-new machine, it's always a good idea to start fresh.

5. Install Design Space. Design Space is "installed" on your computer via a plug-in. It is an addition to your browser of choice (Google Chrome tends to work best). It is what enables the cloud app to run appropriately. Please bear in mind that Design Space is a cloud-based application and therefore does not install or save anything directly onto your computer.

6. You are getting started. You will know that everything is all set when you receive a message prompting you to create your first project. It marks the end of the installation process. You can go ahead and use one of the ready-made projects to help you test out your machine. It's always a good idea to test out various functions to ensure your device is fully operational and does not have any defects. Should things not work well for any reason, contact customer support?

With this, you are now ready to let your imagination fly! Do take the time to become acquainted with Design Space as this is the means that you can use to make your machine come to life.

Installing On Android Or IOS

To install on a mobile device (due to the screen size limitation, a tablet's operation mainly used for a smartphone may be significantly restricted). The installation process works the same as on a computer. The difference lies in the installation of Design Space and the connection of the machine itself.

1. You are pairing your device. The only means to connect your Cricut Machine with a mobile device is via Bluetooth. There is no physical cable that can use. As such, it's essential to make sure that your tablet's Bluetooth is enabled. You can pair the Cricut Machine just like you would any other Bluetooth device.

2. You are downloading the app. To do this, go to your mobile device's app store (Google Play or Apple Store). Do a quick search for Design Space. You will recognize the Cricut logo. It is the app that you need to get. You don't have to purchase the app as it is free to use. Click on "install" and sit tight for a couple of minutes.

3. Create your ID. The app installation process will prompt you to create your Cricut ID. Just follow the steps. If you already have an ID, for instance, when you set up your machine on your computer, sign in with the user and password you created earlier.

4. Setup. Look for the "Machine setup and App Overview" menu. It is the menu that you need to finalize the installation of your machine.

5. New machine. Then, look for "New Machine Setup." Click on this to move the installation process forward.

6. Follow prompts. There is not much else to do here. Just follow the prompts, and you'll be all set to go.

7. You are getting started. You will know that everything is all set when you receive a message prompting you to create your first project. It marks the end of the installation process. You can go ahead and use one of the ready-made projects to help you test out your machine.

Voilà! Your Cricut Machine is now ready for use on a mobile device. It's a good idea to go ahead and set up both your computer and mobile device during the first installation. That way, you are all set to do whatever projects you want on whichever of your instruments. It will give you peace of mind in knowing that you are covered.

One last thing: please make sure to do a test project right away. While this doesn't necessarily mean that you have to do it immediately after finalizing installation, it's always a good idea to do a project to ensure that your machine is working correctly. In case of failure, you can call for a warranty. In this manner, you will feel confident that you won't have any setbacks in working with your brand new Cricut Machine.

Chapter 8. The Business Side of Things and Ideas to Earn

The creativity of your designs and the skill you will develop can allow you to create and start your own business if you wish. For enthusiastic novices, many questions would be faced such as:

1) Where do I start?

Like any start-up business, initial questions need to be addressed to overcome possible difficulties. For example, addressing issues like defining my clientele, the products that might be of interest, where to find them and how to make a profit margin of my sales are important to tackle from the start. In other words, you will need a good and well defined business strategy to start with.

2) Choosing my client

You can target two avenues to sell your products: either by looking at how you can approach the market locally or online. It is advisable to concentrate efforts on one approach to start with as your target is to generate profits as soon as possible. Never forget that your goal is to grow benefit and reinvest it so that your business expands. The quicker you increase your sales, the more likely you will reinvest in new tools or new products, making, in turn, a stronger financial turnover. Understanding your marketing strategy is key to your success.

2.1) Approaching local markets

You can explore selling your products from 'business to business'. In this configuration, the volume of sales is of importance as the larger the production, the lower the production cost per item is. This is the most challenging balance to reach for a new Cricut based business. The advantage of obtaining contractual work means you can negotiate to buy a large quantity from vendors. However, such 'golden' opportunities are hard to find since such contracts are opened to competition. Yet, as a new start-up business, you can present your products specifically tailored for business customers. A custom work approach offers positive aspects as businesses always look for originality and good products. By creating such a relationship, your business is likely to become a point of reference for future other contacts, hence launching many opportunities for upselling. However, it is important to bear in mind that finding such niche is hard as competition is very stiff!

Another approach to consider for selling your products is from 'business to customer'. In this model, though the volume of sales remains important, your objective is to present your products to retail customers willing to buy them. Creativity, imagination will be keys to your success, as well as what type of media and medium you want to work in (e.g. T-shirts, mugs). Equally important is a retail space you will need to choose to offer your items. Experiencing different locations and products is all part of the efforts of a new start-up business. Also, a custom work approach for local customers will present advantages since the startup cost are the lowest of all the different strategies described so far. However, as a new business in the field, starting can be difficult. Word of mouth can be your first step as well as producing good products at an affordable price.

2.2) Selling Online

If you are an adept of higher technical knowledge, then you can generate great benefits by providing either quality custom work, bulk offering or information network. It is advisable to concentrate your efforts on one approach to start with. If you choose, for example, a custom work approach, you increase the chances to find potential customers looking for your products as they turn to a search engine like Google to find what they are looking for. Websites like Amazon Handmade or Etsy provide a good platform to allow selling custom design services. Equally efficient is the launch of your site. This strategy is worth looking at. Selling online presents advantages such as low startup costs and access to the global market with access to millions of potential customers. Furthermore, online custom prices tend to be lower than those on the local market. However, access to the global market means that competition is stiff, pushing products to be competitively priced. Selling online requires certain knowledge in logistics as far as shipping and packing your products are concerned, a cost factor that needs to be taken into consideration in your pricing.

EBay and Amazon have become the largest platforms. On the other hand, if an online retail business approach is more what you may be inclined to do, then this approach will give you the ability to determine the demand for the designs you offer and plan the production accordingly. But selling online means challenging the existing competition!

Finally, if you prefer to sell your products online through information network, then you become an authority in the field, creating the opportunity to generate profit with your Cricut designs. By offering blogs on technical know-how or inspiration work, you become selective on the posts you want to take on.

Starting a new business requires foremost a business strategy, the foundation for your future success. Asking yourself who your potential customers would be, what kind of products you can sell them and how are the first steps of a future startup business.

In terms of making money from the comfort of your home, you easily achieve that with a Cricut machine. However, you have to bear in mind that there are a number of competitors out there, thus you have to put in extra efforts in order to stand a chance to succeed.

For you to become successful in the Cricut world of crafts, you have to keep the following in mind;

1. Dare to be different

You have to be yourself, unleash your quirkiness and creativity.

Those that have been in the Cricut crafts world for some time know all about the knockout name tiles. They became a hit and in no time, everyone was producing and selling them.

In the crafting world, that is the norm. Thus, you could be among the earliest people to jump on a trend to ride the wave until the next hot seller surfaces. Mind you, that strategy of selling Cricut crafts can become costly and tiresome if you are not careful.

The basic idea here is to add your flair and personal style, and not to completely re-invent the wheel. For example, let's say you come across two name tiles on Etsy, one looks exactly like the other 200+ on sale on the site, while the second one has a few more tweaks and spins on it. The seller of the second product will possibly charge more and accrue a higher profit because his/her product is unique and stands out from the rest.

When you design your products, don't be afraid to tweak your fonts, because even the simplest of tweaks and creativity can make your product stand out from the rest.

Remember this; if you create a product that looks exactly like others, you are only putting yourself in a 'price war', where no one usually wins.

2. Keep it narrow

A lot of crafters out there believe that creating and selling everything under the sun translates into more patronage, and more money, but that isn't how it works. On the contrary, it might only result in a huge stock of unsold products, more burn out and heavy cost. Rather than producing materials here and there, you should focus on being the best in your area of craftiness, so that when people need specific products in your area, they'll come to you.

It can be very tempting to want to spread your tentacles because it might seem like the more you produce, the more options you'll provide for your clients, but that might be counterproductive.

Take out time to think about your area of strength and focus your energy on making products that you'd be known for. It is better to be known as an expert in a particular product than to be renowned for someone that produces a high number of inferior products.

Thus, you should keep it narrow and grow to become the very best in your area of craft.

3. be consistent

If you intend to become successful, you have to work on your Cricut craft business consistently. Some people work once a week or thereabout because they sell as a hobby; however, if you intend to make in-road in your business, you have to work every day.

If you have other engagements and can't work every day, then you should create a weekly schedule and stick to it. If you shun your business for weeks and months at a time, then you will not go anywhere with it.

Apart from consistency in work and production, you also have to be consistent with your product quality and pricing. When your customers are convinced about your products, they will easily recommend you to their friends, family, business partners, and many others.

In business, there are ups and downs, thus, you shouldn't reduce your work rate because things are not going as planned. Success doesn't come easy, but one of the surest ways of being and maintaining success is by consistently doing the things you love.

4. Be Tenacious

It is not easy to run a business because it involves a lot of hard work, sweat, and even heartbreaks. Thus, you have to bear in mind that there will be days when you will feel like throwing in the towel. There will be days when nothing go as planned. There will also be days when customers will tick you off. You will feel like a drowning boat because you're working hard but nothing is working out.

However, you have to look at the bigger picture, because the crafting business is not a get rich quick scheme. Remember, quitters never win, so quitting isn't an option. Keep doing the things you love, and keep improving. Successful people never give up. They suffer many setbacks but they don't stop.

Thus, for you to be successful in your craft, you have to be tenacious and resilient. Be willing to maneuver your way through tough times, and do not forget to pick up lessons.

5. Learn everyday

Be willing to learn from people that have been successful in the business. You don't necessarily have to unravel everything by yourself, because whatever it is you are doing, others have already done it in the past.

Whether you intend to learn how to build a successful Facebook group or how to go up the Etsy ranks, remember that people have already done all that in the past, and are giving out tricks and tips they know.

Make it a tradition to learn something new about your business every day because, at the beginning of your business, you will have to do more marketing than crafting.

When you wake up in the morning, browse through the internet, gather materials and read at your spare time, because the more you learn the better your chances of being successful. They say knowledge is power, and for you to become successful as a craftsman/woman, you have to constantly seek new knowledge in the form of tips, tricks, software upgrades, marketing, design ideas, tools, accessories, and many others. All I am saying is that you should learn without ceasing.

Chapter 9. Creative Ideas to Do on Your Cricut

Now that you know what a Cricut machine is and how to set it up, it is now time to delve into the best part of the Cricut— making your designs! We will look at the materials that you can use, what can be cut, and what crafts can be made. In all honest— the options are endless as crafters are constantly coming up with new ideas and new craft using the Cricut, so each time, you'll find something new.

Cricut Paper Crafts

What do you need? You need some standard weight paper, or you can also use cardstock. Cricut has both these options which you can purchase. You can use this, or you can use any paper you like. Here is a selection of ideas that you can kick start your Cricut paper crafts. Just click on the links of the specific craft to get more details:

• Creating a 3D Paper Bouquet

Cricut is an excellent tool to make beautiful, one-of-a-kind paper bouquets simply because they have plenty of flower patterns you can choose from. You can make these paper bouquets using paper of any kind and in any color. Using different hues from the same color would be ideal because it gives you depth and texture.

- No-Sew Paper Garland

See all these amazing paper garlands during weddings and events? How do people do this many garlands? Well, they probably used the Cricut. No-sew paper garlands brighten up any space and you can use different kinds of shapes to create your garlands. Once you cut it out using your Cricut, all you need to do is string thread through these cut-outs and hang them up. That's how it's done!

- Personalized Napkin Rings

If you do not have a design in mind to make your napkin rings, head over to the Cricut Design Space, type in 'napkin rings,' and you'll find a host of designs that you can tweak and use to your liking. Making your napkin rings with initials or even images of your own to make your event personalized.

- How to Make 3D Flowers

Cricut flowers, while beautiful, can be a little tedious and tough to assemble. Thankfully, this handy, step-by-step guide provided by Hey Let's Make Stuff is useful for crafters looking to add some paper floral arrangements to their dining table centerpiece, a mantel, or decoration on a wedding vase.

- Lampshade

This craft requires you to work on an existing lampshade and upgrade it. All you need is a lampshade that has seen better days and think about you want to redecorate it. You can paint the lampshade with fabric paint and then print out different motifs, such as butterflies to paste on the lampshade, to give it a beautiful 3D effect.

- Paper Marigolds

Take your decoration game to the next level with Cricut. Put on a glorious show for the Day of the Dead by taking out your Cricut and making beautiful yellow and orange marigold paper flowers. With the Cricut, you can make these paper flowers as realistic as can be and as big and bold as you want it to be. Making paper flowers large, and as many as possible, will be easily done with the Cricut. The hardest part is assembling them according to its sizes.

- Notebook Revamp with the Cricut

With some black vinyl and notebooks that you have lying around, you can amp up your notebooks to the next level. How? Use the Cricut on its vinyl settings, place your black vinyl on the grip mat, and get to work. By the end of the day, you can have a bunch of fashionable, black-letter notebooks worthy of being in a bookstore.

- Paper Swag

This paper swag can be any motifs you like, but leaf motifs are among the favorites. Find a leaf collage on the Cricut Design Space, cut the motifs out, and use a scoring tool to score a line straight to the middle of the leaf to fold on the lines. You can use floral tape and wire to secure leaves, and use ribbons or any other adornments to make the swag beautiful.

- Paper Succulent Centerpieces

Don't like gardening but still like the look of succulents? The Happy Scraps has an amazing tutorial on how you can create a paper succulent centerpiece. Cricut even has succulent colored cardstock, which you can use to create this look exactly the way Happy Scraps has done. Make these flowers and place them the way a succulent garden would look—in a nice container.

- Pop-Up Cards

If you love making cards and giving them to your near and dear or even selling them on your Etsy store, then investing in a Cricut is the way to go. You can make pop-up cards of any kind and any cardstock. All you need is a little bit of creativity. Like this pop-up rainbow card, it is so versatile you can make it any motifs such as shades of red hearts for Valentine's Day, snowflakes for Christmas greeting cards, four-leaf clover shapes for St. Patrick's Day, or even book shaped motifs where you can add in your favorite short quotes.

- Luminaries

Do you ever look at luminaries and think 'How beautiful they are' and wonder how those intricate paper carvings were done? Luminaries are great for the holidays or for table centerpieces at a restaurant, and they are among the popular decorations for weddings as well, to light up the aisle, as table decorations, and so on. In this tutorial by Jennifer Maker, she uses layers of beautifully cut panels to provide contrast and texture. You need vellum to complete your luminaries, and also because this is paper—do not use candles, but LED candles would be a better and safer option.

- Cricut Vinyl Crafts

One of the most common projects plenty crafters choose to work on is with vinyl with the Cricut. Cricut offers an amazing variety of vinyl to choose from, and they are all in excellent quality. You can get the standard vinyl, more premium ones, glitter vinyls that are the crowd favorite, printable vinyls, dry erase ones, and chalkboard vinyls. Here is a selection of things you can do with them:

- Pantry Labels

This craft idea makes for an amazing beginner's craft. Labels are one of the easiest things to make with the Cricut and the most straightforward. All you need for this is Vinyl, transfer tape, label designs that you can get from the Cricut Design App, and your machine.

- Vinyl Board

You can use any board to create a vinyl of words or images to update your board. Using chalkboard is one of the favorites as it creates a nice decor for the home. You can cut out words from your vinyl and stick it on to your board. It can say 'Welcome Home,' or 'Grocery List,' or even a motivational quote.

- DIY Drink Coasters

Coasters are another kind of beginner's craft to do with your Cricut. You can personalize it any way you want, such as using fonts, images, colors, or glitter vinyl—the options are endless. You need a standard grip mat to work with, the basic cricut tools, the type of vinyl you want to use, and some transfer tape. Of course, your choice of coasters is also essential for this project, so don't forget this. Clear varnish is also needed to finish the project.

- Playroom Accent Wall

This accent wall for your child's playroom makes a colorful statement to brighten up your kid's day. The most tedious part of this project would be measuring and painting the wall. After that, the fun part begins with the Cricut machine to do fun decorations. The basic Cricut Essential Tool set is a must to have in vinyl projects as it makes taking out intricate cuts out smoothly and easily.

- Memory Game

This is a fun kid's craft project that uses a vibrant lime vinyl. In this craft, you make tiles featuring animal images. Cricut released its Cricut Vinyl Brights which includes 12" x 12" sheets of vinyl in vibrant colors from Grape, Sunshine, Caribbean, Lime, Flamingo, and Azure. These colors are fun which is perfect for summer crafts.

- Chalkboard Robot Town

If you want to color up and decorate your children's room walls, using Cricut Vinyl for wall decals makes decorating these walls easy. All you need to do is design or find symbols that you like, resize it to the size you want to fit your walls, cut it, weed it, and stick it. For projects involving murals, it is always best to measure your space and create a design on your Design Space App, placing the motifs or symbols or images to where you envision it on the wall, on your canvas in the app.

Once you are happy with what you have, connect it to the Cricut, cut it out, weed it out, and then start sticking.

- Personalized Sports Gear

Yes, you can your sports gear scream your name! Have you joined a group workout or sports clubs and brought your gear along only to find it's gone missing because someone mistook your stuff for theirs? Well, if you have ever found yourself in a situation like this, it's best to get your gear emblazoned with your name on it, so nobody mistakenly takes it again. This is a perfect idea for your luggage too. Use the vinyl Cricut settings to create your name with an image of your choice—anything that stands out against the color of the object you want to personalize so it is visible and it can be spotted from a distance.

- Holographic Phone Case

If you are one of those people who love changing your phone cases, the Cricut makes it possible for you to have every season or whenever you feel a change coming your way—except with half the cost and exactly the way you want it to look. Holographic cases have become quite popular, and Cricut crafters have a bunch of tutorials and SVG files that you can use, like this one from Laura's Crafty Life. To do this project, you would need a clear phone case of course that suits your phone size, as well as holographic vinyl. Explore the designs you like to use and use your Cricut to make this happen.

- Decorated Vinyl Flower Pots

If you love keeping plants and have a few indoor plants all around your home, time to give them an upgrade by adding some fun motifs to your pots. Some people add intricate designs, some add gold bands to give it some extra class, some put on labels, and some just put on fun motifs. You can use any vinyl that fits your creative ideas and use your Cricut to get this idea to reality.

- Cricut Iron-On Crafts

Another must-do and popular craft among the Cricut fraternity is the iron-on. Iron-ons are among the most popular after paper or even vinyl crafts simply because you can use it on everything from wood ornaments to T-Shirts, jeans, tote bags, and onesies. You can even make your holiday gifts with the Cricut Iron-On crafts for your family and friends.

Conclusion

Thank you for making it to the end. I think every enthusiastic crafter should invest in at least one of the Cricut products mentioned. If you have to add up all the time spent on perfecting lettering and cutting out intricate designs, patterns and slicing fondant with those pesky blades by hand. While there's nothing that beats homemade products, cards or personalized coasters, you can still personalize the same things with any of the Cricut machines and have the change to give them a professional and clean finish.

I have made hundreds of projects with my Cricut, and I am still learning every single day. It is like a computer; you will never learn every little trick in one goes. You will have to practice, follow the guide I have given, and add or scratch ideas out until you have your own Tomorrow I might learn something new, and I will kick myself for not adding that to this guide. Nevertheless, know that I have taught you every trick I know and shared every failure I have encountered in hopes that you can avoid it all and just start crafting like we all so desperately have wanted to do when we first got our Cricuts.

Never stop doing research. Never stop trying new things. Never, ever stop being creative. The Cricut does not make you any less creative; it just makes the process easier and efforts on more important things or personalizing the projects after making the cuts. It takes the tedious work out of your hands and makes everything fun, easy, and fast.

When in regards to arts and crafts, so you may never fail with Cricut Cartridges. In order to get many of years, lots of aspiring artists are inspired by different layouts and patterns offered by the capsules created by Cricut. Regular, a great deal of shops can market a small number of capsules because of growing demand of those products as soon as it comes to neighborhood shops. With the popularity of this line, a great deal of retailers also has been effective in leasing to your brand. For people that aren't into arts and crafts, then you might not understand a whole lot about Cricut capsules. But, we guarantee you that understanding more about those products can help yourself participate in more activities concerning paper crafts.

The finest thing concerning Cricut cartridges is that you don't ever appear to run out of ideas and choices. Whether you adore fonts, shapes or animation characters, you'll have the ability to locate a cartridge which can fit your taste. But when choosing a cartridge out of Cricut, the very first thing which you will need to take into account is how far your budget will probably be. The selection of costs of these capsules can appear as low as just a bit below fifty dollars, and may soar alongside a hundred bucks.

If you're the sort of person who enjoys a great deal of colors, you are able to stick with the fundamental silhouette cartridges and just take advantage of different colored papers to perform your cutouts. If you would rather create use of words, then state for the scrapbook designs, you might even use the ribbon cartridges. Additionally, there are people who are a massive fan of this certified character collection. I hope you have learned something!